THE CIVIL WAR IN LANCASHIRE

BY STEPHEN BULL

Lancashire County Books, 1991

THE CIVIL WAR IN LANCASHIRE

by Stephen Bull

942.76

04827968

PL 7.91

Published by Lancashire County Books, 143 Corporation Street, Preston
(a Lancashire County Museums production)

First edition, April 1991

British Library Cataloguing in Publication Data
Bull, Stephen
    The civil war in Lancashire
    1. Lancashire (England). Civil wars
    I. Title
    942.76062

ISBN 1-871236-00-2

Typeset by Carnegie Publishing Ltd., Maynard Street, Preston
Printed by Pindar Graphics (Preston) Ltd., 1 Garstang Road, Preston

Contents

Acknowledgements

This booklet was first produced to accompany an exhibition of the same title at the Lancashire County and Regimental Museum at Preston, commemorating the 350th anniversary of the outbreak of the civil wars.

In addition to those persons and institutions noted in the picture captions the author would especially like to thank the Library, Museums and Arts Committee of Lancashire County Council; Lord Shuttleworth; Mr John Blundell, County Museums Officer, as well as all of his colleagues; the Lancashire Record Office; also Anne Barlow, Keith Matthews, Sally Coleman, Stephen Whittle, Peter Christmas, Stuart Read, Robert Sharman, Mike Seed and several private collectors who prefer to remain anonymous. The staffs of Towneley Hall, Burnley; Blackburn Museum; Wigan B.C.; National Museums and Galleries on Merseyside; the Royal Armouries; Lancaster University; Warrington Museum, and the Museums and Galleries Commission, must be thanked collectively. Similar thanks go to every member of Hoghton's regiment of foot (Sealed Knot).

Stephen Bull, County and Regimental Museum, 1991

Johan Blaeu's map of Lancashire, 1648.

One

SEVENTEENTH-CENTURY

LANCASHIRE

Land and Communication

L ANCASHIRE was a very different place 350 years ago. The old county was much larger than today, taking in the regions of Furness to the north and the areas which now make up most of Merseyside and Greater Manchester to the south. Warrington and a small portion of what is now Cheshire were also part of the county.

Lancashire was mainly rural with a population of only around 150,000. There was a good deal of arable land in the central and southern parts of the county, but to the west, north and east much of the land was unsuitable for crops. On the coast were large areas of undrained marsh and moss which provided turf and some grazing. In the higher land of the Pennines to the east, cattle for meat and dairy predominated.

Such industry as did exist was concentrated mainly in the south east of the county, where small-scale spinning and weaving enterprises had already begun. Some iron and copper work was done in Lonsdale, but the county was still overwhelmingly rural, with no more than ten per cent of the population living in towns. Manchester was the largest with a little over 4,000 people, while Preston and Wigan had around half that figure each. Bolton, Bury, Blackburn, Rochdale, Lancaster, Warrington, Salford and Liverpool can have had little more than 1,000.

Communications were very rudimentary; the fastest methods of movement were by sea or on horseback, but the marshlands of the west and the hills of the east, coupled with indifferent roads, made progress slow over land. A form of postal service existed, mainly for official documents, but low levels of literacy would in any case have restricted written communication. There were newspapers or broadsheets and, as today, these varied in quality from the sensational and scurrilous to more considered journals.

A few people did travel great distances, notably the rich, lawyers, soldiers and some clergy, but predominantly the outlook was parochial. Most Englishmen referred to their county as their 'country' and the local landowner and county officials were more important in everyday life than either king or parliament. Most people born within the county would marry and die in it, some of them of the periodic plagues that were still a recurring problem.

Religion

IN terms of religion most Lancastrians were fairly old-fashioned in their views. Their forbears had largely disagreed with the Reformation and had seen no very good reason to depart from the traditional ways; in the mid-seventeenth century many people, especially in the west of Lancashire, yet remained Catholics. In the north of the county religious provision of any sort was scanty; in one case an old man interviewed by a puritan minister in 1644 protested that he had heard of Jesus Christ only once, at a Corpus Christi play at Kendal. Only in the south east of the county was there a more fundamental and Protestant approach to religion, and here the commercial links between centres like Manchester or Bolton and the south east of England seem to have fostered more progressive, Protestant religious views. There seems to have been a link between greater prosperity, industry, and puritanism.

Administration and power

LANCASHIRE was divided into six 'hundreds'. The largest of these was in the south west of the county: West Derby, which stretched across a wide, mainly rural area and encompassed the towns of Wigan, Warrington and Liverpool. Salford Hundred included most of the industrial areas of the south east of the county and stretched as far as the River Mersey and the Yorkshire border. In the centre of the county were Amounderness, Leyland and Blackburn hundreds and, to the north, Lonsdale. Lonsdale was certainly the most backward, divided into two by Morecambe Bay and with its administrative centre at Lancaster.

Lancashire returned fourteen members to parliament, two representing the county as a whole and two each for the boroughs of Lancaster, Preston, Clitheroe, Wigan, Newton and Liverpool. In 1642, shortly before the outbreak of the civil war, these were divided eight to six in favour of parliament. Voting in elections was confined to male property holders of a certain standing and was very restricted. At the 1640 election in Clitheroe, for example, there were only 83 voters who between them returned two MPs.

Top of the local hierarchy and automatically entitled to a seat in the House of Lords were the peers. Lancashire's three peers in 1642 were James Stanley, Lord Strange (later seventh Earl of Derby); Viscount Richard Molyneux of Sefton; and Henry Lord Morley and Mounteagle. The Earl of Derby was the most important and active in the royalist cause but all three peers supported the king in the civil war. A little under eight hundred county families claimed 'gentry' status. Half of these men appear to have played little part in the conflict and can probably best be described as neutral, whilst 200 actively supported the king and 100 parliament.

There was no standing army in 1642; instead, the militia was called out and put on a semi-permanent footing when the need arose. Local gentlemen received the 'king's commission' and established regiments of infantry or troops of horse accord-ingly. These were usually known by the name of their colonel.

For the maintenance of law and order there was no organised police force but each locality had its own justices of the peace and constables. The former acted as magistrates; the latter actually brought the wrong-doers before them. There was a fairly well developed legal system locally. Most minor matters at township or village level were either settled more or less amicably within the local community or were heard before the 'courts leet'. More important matters were discussed and tried at the three-monthly 'quarter sessions', held at Lancaster, Preston, Manchester and (alternately) Wigan and Ormskirk; at these sessions the justices of the peace had very wide-ranging powers to investigate crimes, misdemeanours and breaches of local regulations, as well as conducting most of the overall administration of county affairs. The most serious crimes, and by 1600 all capital offences, were tried in front of justices of assize in Lancaster twice a year. On top of this were various courts of inquiry and Church courts at a local level, whilst, as today, the final court of appeal was the Lords.

Two

CIVIL WAR, 1642–6

Causes of the Civil War

THE causes of the wars which raged intermittently between 1642 and 1651 and ultimately took in Ireland, Scotland and Wales, have been long debated. They have been portrayed in terms of a simple power struggle between king and parliament; a religious conflict of Catholic against Protestant; and as a small part of a much more general Europe-wide crisis in which prices, armies and navies outran the states' ability to tax and administer.

What is certain is that the causes of the civil wars were both national and local, and that longer-term grievances and problems were suddenly brought to a head by a financial crisis which necessitated the re-call of parliament in 1640 after a gap of eleven years, and made worse by open rebellion in Scotland and Ireland. Last-minute concessions from King Charles I, including the abandonment of his unpopular adviser and minister, the Earl of Strafford, and some of his more controversial schemes, split the country in 1641.

National Causes

Since the previous reign, of James I, the monarchy had suffered a series of financial difficulties. Military forces were particularly expensive to recruit and maintain and the king could only raise ordinary revenue with the sanction and consent of parliament, which represented the country as a whole. In return, parliament demanded a say in matters of religion, administration and even foreign policy as their price. To avoid this the Stuart monarchs then sought 'extraordinary' means of raising money. This took many and varied forms – 'tonnage and poundage' on trade; 'ship money' levied on coastal counties and then on the whole country, ostensibly to support the navy; monopolies granted by the king in turn for fees; and hosts of minor annoying fees and fines on forests, feudal rights, knighthood, and even currants!

In the religious sphere the official Church of England, with its bishops appointed by the king, was seen by many in parliament and the country as a whole to be moving closer to Catholicism under 'Arminian' reformers like Archbishop Laud. In 1639 and 1640 the Church had already become a major factor in the so-called Bishops' Wars between England and Scotland. Since Charles I was king of both countries, civil war of a sort was already happening, especially since parliament and those of a 'puritan' persuasion in religion showed sympathy with the Scottish point of view.

Local Causes

It seems that whilst national events were the main 'causes' of the war local factors were often very important in deciding individual sympathies. In Lancashire most Catholics, all of the peers and some two-thirds of the active gentry took the side of the king with greater or lesser degrees of enthusiasm. Although a slim majority of the county's MPs showed allegiance to the parliamentarian cause, the overwhelming impression was of a royalist county.

The final breaking point was the issuing by parliament and king of rival 'militia ordinances' and 'commissions of array': parliament claimed the right to control the militia and, fearing that the king would use armed force against them, made a call to arms in its defence under the so-called 'Militia Ordinance'. Charles, condemning these actions of parliament as rebellious, called out the militia under his own authority using the time-honoured method of sending out Commissioners of Array. After this both sides, in Lancashire as elsewhere, attempted to seize strongholds, magazines and munitions.

A 1644 five-shilling piece showing King Charles I on horseback. Parliament's control of the capital led Charles to make his base at Oxford, where this coin was issued. Electrotype by Seaby's of London.

Three

WARFARE IN

SEVENTEENTH-CENTURY

ENGLAND

THANKS to many surviving objects, books and manuscript accounts it is possible to obtain a good idea of what warfare was like during the civil wars.

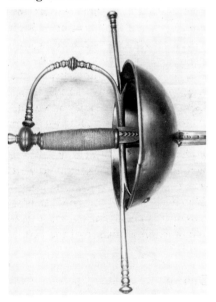

A continental cup hilt rapier of the early-17th century. From the collection at Turton Tower, Lancashire.

It is a popular misconception that royalists and parliamentarians dressed and acted very differently. Largely this was not the case. Though some 'cavaliers' may have dressed and acted flamboyantly and some gentlemen of 'puritan' persuasion may have adopted short hair and sober clothing, these images were probably caricatures that the two sides drew of each other for propaganda purposes.

For the most part the arms and equipment of the two sides were similar. A good deal of it came from magazines of the militia or 'trained bands', some from noble armouries. Only later did parliament's control of the sea, and London arms production, begin to show itself in better equipped armies.

Both sides deployed several armies. Some were made up of local militias or gathered by prominent noblemen for the defence of a county or locality – others were 'national' in the sense that they were paid directly by king or parliament and intended

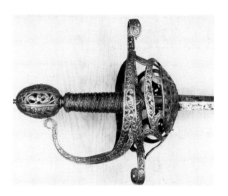

English rapier of around 1630, with swept hilt and hollow, chiselled pommel and wire grip. York Castle Museum.

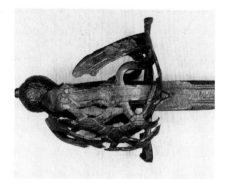

Mid-17th-century basket-hilted broad sword found in the brook at Woodplumpton. Private local collection.

for use all over the country. Additionally both sides deployed many garrisons to hold important towns or strong points.

Infantry

The armies were divided into three 'arms' – infantry, cavalry, and artillery. Infantry were the most numerous and the basic unit was the regiment commanded by a colonel. These regiments were notionally over 1,000-strong, but casualties and poor recruiting could often leave them much weaker.

Each regiment contained pikemen and musketeers. The former were the biggest men, armed with 16- or 18-foot pikes. The musketeers were armed with smooth-bore matchlock muskets, whose powder was ignited simply by a smouldering matchcord held in the moving 'serpent' of the lock. Rifled weapons and flint-locks were not unknown but were limited in numbers and tended to be used by skirmishers, sentinels and officers.

The main bodies of infantry were usually drawn up with pikes in the centre and musketeers on the wings. The pikes held off cavalry or attempted to close with the enemy whilst the musketeers relied on their firepower, discharging rank by rank and falling back to reload. The tactics used were either based on the traditional 'Dutch' system, the more modern 'Swedish' with its smaller, more flexible units, or a mixture of the two.

Cavalry

Cavalry, the most prestigious arm, was still numerous in English forces. Regiments were deployed, especially

A musketeer loading his weapon. From Jacob de Gheyn's 'Exercise of Arms', 1607.

later in the war, but the basic unit was often the troop of about 70 men. Most cavalry were equipped with breast- and back-plate and a barred 'pot' helmet, though some wore the thick leather 'buff' coat. Swords, pistols and sometimes carbines were carried. Cavalry firearms were usually either wheel-locks or doglocks in which a spark was struck, since managing a matchcord was virtually impossible on horseback. It is a mistake to think that the 'pot' helmet was only ever used by parliamentarians and that buff and armour were always worn together. There is no real evidence for either opinion.

Other types of cavalry were the 'cuirassiers', armoured from head to knee, and the lancer, normally used by the Scots. The 'dragoon' was not really a cavalryman but an infantryman who used a horse to reach the battlefield and dismounted to fight with firearms.

Cavalry tactics varied; in the traditional system they rode up close, discharged their weapons and fell back waiting their opportunity to charge a demoralised or disorganised unit. More recent theory suggested charging home directly with the sword; when this worked it was spectacular but it was seldom successful against formed pikemen.

Artillery

There were two main types of artillery, heavy siege guns and lighter field guns. Both were effective in their place but they were often hampered by transport and supply problems. Even the lightest guns had a range of over half a mile and the ability to cut through several ranks of men.

Artillery was organised in 'trains' allotted to each field or besieging army or to town defences; a few guns sometimes travelled with each infantry regiment. Mortars with their exploding shells or 'grenadoes' were rare but terrifying weapons most effective in sieges. Other artillery used solid ball or 'case' shot of many projectiles in a single container.

Siege and battle

In the ideal battlefield disposition the infantry formed the core of the army, the regiments being deployed in two or more major lines. Cavalry occupied either flank, and guns the front. Ideally the whole force would be on or behind a ridge line with only a few skirmishers and artillery pieces to the front, concealing the strength of the force and its intentions to the enemy.

In smaller actions this sound plan was rarely adhered to, fights developing around bridges, strongpoints and patrols. In siege situations the attackers were usually stronger than the defence and dug 'lines' around the besieged town or castle. Artillery could then be brought forward to 'breach' the enemy defence. If they did not surrender they were then 'stormed' by the infantry, engineers, or dismounted cavalry, who went in with edged weapons, grenades and pikes.

Lord Strange, later 7th Earl of Derby, with his wife Charlotte, the defender of Lathom House, and his daughter. 19th-century engraving. By permission of E. Winder.

Four

THE COURSE OF THE
WAR IN LANCASHIRE

IN February 1642 parliament nominated Lord Wharton as Lord Lieutenant for Lancashire whilst Lord Strange was nominated by the king for the same post for both Lancashire and Cheshire. Neither side wanted open hostilities to break out, however, and both petitioned the king and parliament seeking redress of local grievances and suggesting accommodations whereby war could be avoided. Parliament's supporters in Lancashire looked on with great concern at the mounting rebellion in Ireland and for several weeks were extremely afraid of an invasion by Irish Catholic forces:

Being seated in the mouthe of danger, and having fresh and daily spectacles of the Irish cruelties presented to their eyes, cannot but chuse but apprehend feare from the noveltie of so great barbarism and lest that kingdom . . . being lost the war . . . should be transported hither from the opposite shore, where the number of Popish Recusants, and the opportunity of landing, may invite an invasion.

Despite the fact that many people remained neutral, royalist and parliamentarian activists now began to gather forces.

In June Lord Strange called a meeting of royalist supporters on Fulwood Moor, near Preston. Many of the opposition turned up as well, including the parliamentarians Alexander Rigby and Richard Shuttleworth, and the result was a shouting match with both sides attempting to read rival declarations. At the same time the royalists seized control of the magazine. In answer parliamentarian supporters secured Manchester and its munitions. On July 15th Lord Strange himself went to Manchester, with predictable consequences; shooting started and a man who pulled a royalist gentleman from his horse was shot – Richard Perceval of Kirkmanshulme thus becoming Lancashire's first fatality.

After this the battle lines became more sharply drawn. West Derby, Leyland, Amounderness and Lonsdale supported the king, Salford Hundred was for parliament. Blackburn Hundred, initially neutral, subsequently sided with parliament.

The Siege of Manchester, 1642

THINGS initially went very well for the royalists. They seized the majority of the county's arms and munitions and controlled all the castles and strongpoints. Only parliamentarian Manchester held out against the king.

Lord Strange succeeded his father, as seventh Earl of Derby, in September 1642, and that month decided to seize Manchester, which would have had the effect of turning Lancashire into a royalist powerbase. Already, however, the Mancunians were organising themselves, directed by the local 'committee' and with the aid of an experienced German mercenary officer, Colonel John Rosworm. Earth ramparts were erected and the street ends were blocked using chains. The total number of the defenders was about 1,000, gathered not only from south-east Lancashire but northern Cheshire as well. Their best units were the local militia under Captain Radcliffe and 150 tenants of Mr. Assheton of Middleton, commanded by Captain Bradshaw.

Lord Derby with his army of 2,000 infantry, 500 cavalry and half a dozen

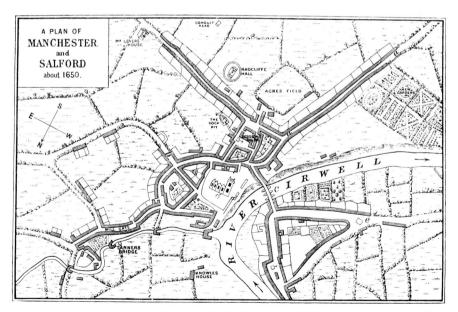

Manchester and Salford in around 1650.

15

Alexander Rigby, one of the most prominent of the parliamentarians in Lancashire.

John Rosworm, the defender of Manchester.

guns left Warrington on 24th September and arrived before Manchester early on the 26th. First he called on the town to surrender; this was refused and so a bombardment was begun at noon. Later the same afternoon attacks were made against Deansgate and over Salford Bridge. This assault was bloodily repulsed. The next day the royalists fired on Manchester from Salford and a fresh attack was launched on Market Stead Lane, again unsuccessfully. Further appeals for surrender were refused and skirmishing continued until 1st October, when Lord Derby, unable to break Manchester's resolution, decided to give up and retreat. He had lost over a hundred men and Captain Standish of Duxbury.

Less than a month later the king's main field army met the parliamentarian army of the Earl of Essex at Edgehill in Warwickshire. The royalists were fought to a standstill and prevented from reaching the capital. The chance of a swift royalist victory was gone, both nationally and locally.

In November Sir Gilbert Hoghton of Hoghton Tower did manage to seize Blackburn for the king. He held it only briefly, however, for the local parliamentarian leaders Colonels Shuttleworth and Starkie at the head of almost 8,000 men succeeded in driving him out. A few days later, on 27th November, another skirmish took place at Chowbent and the royalists were again worsted.

In the meantime fighting had also broken out in the Wigan area, the local parliamentarian company being supported by two more from Manchester. In the first action Captains Bradshaw and Venables were captured but on Christmas Eve reinforcements from Manchester reached Leigh, marching on the market place from several directions and managing to seize many of the royalists' arms.

Parliament gains control of the county

THE Manchester parliamentarians were quick to appoint a new leader, Sir John Seaton, and to increase their forces for an aggressive campaign in the New Year. The first major action was a combined attack by Sir John and Colonel Shuttleworth on Preston. The first assault was made at dawn on 9th February, but the numerically weaker royalists made a fight of it and it was two hours before the parliamentarians had subdued all resistance.

After this royalist lines of communication west of the Pennines were severely disrupted and the way was clear for further parliamentarian advances in the county, despite the fact that the king was doing reasonably well in other parts of England.

Pikeman's armour, made by the London Armourers Company, from the York Castle Museum collection.

Pike officer's morion of the early-17th century. From York Castle Museum.

Hoghton Tower fell next, captured bloodlessly by Colonel Starkie. However, an accidental explosion killed him and some of his men after they had entered. The royalists replied with a determined assault on Bolton with eleven companies of foot and two troops each of dragoons and horse. The five hundred defenders were outnumbered, but although the royalists surrounded the town and fought fierce actions with troops manning the outposts, they were ultimately unsuccessful. One weapon used by the attackers which we would now call a 'Morgen Stern' or 'Morning Star' was described in the contemporary tract *Lancashire's Valley of Achor* in the following terms:

> An head about a quarter of a yard long, a staffe of two yards long, or more, put into that head, twelve iron pikes round about, and one in the end to stab with. This fierce weapon . . . they called a Roundhead.

In early March 1643 occurred one of the most curious events of the whole war. A Spanish ship, the *Santa Anna*, apparently became hopelessly lost before grounding on the Fylde coast near Rossall Point in the mouth of the Wyre. Initially she was boarded and claimed by local parliamentarians. The Earl of Derby at Lathom heard of the incident and rapidly set off for the spot with a troop of horse. Meanwhile four companies of parliamentarian foot set out from Preston to reinforce the captors of the ship.

The parliamentarians had a head start of fifteen miles but hearing that Derby was in the area when they were near Poulton they retreated behind the Wyre and Derby's cavalry won the race. He burned the ship, took some prisoners, including the parliamentarian Colonel Doddington, and rode rapidly south again. The saga was not over yet, however, because the parliamentarians were still able to salvage the ship's cannon and the Spanish ambassador intervened on behalf of the crew in an attempt to get them taken back to Flanders.

Lord Derby now began to formulate a plan to capture the Spanish ship's guns, apparently 22 in number, which had been taken to Lancaster. To this end he gathered 1,000 of his own men and marched from Wigan to the Fylde where he was joined by 3,000 local sympathisers and a much more organised body of troops numbering 600 which Sir John Girlington had brought from York.

Outnumbering the defenders by about nine to one the royalists burst into Lancaster, plundering and burning the town. A number of parliamentarians, including Captain William Shuttleworth, were killed and others took refuge in the castle. The parliamentarians now sent belated support under Colonels Assheton and Seaton but they were outwitted as the royalists slipped past them on the road south of the town. Derby quickly marched to Preston, which had been left but poorly defended, and re-captured that town for the king, apparently with some help from the royalist supporters amongst its population.

Spectacular though this march had been, the success was short-lived. Derby again failed to take Bolton in an attack at the end of March and a parliamentarian force of 2,000 commanded by Colonels Holland and Rosworm stormed Wigan, inflicting heavy casualties and plundering the town. Next the parliamentarians attacked Warrington in the company of their Cheshire compatriot, Sir William Brereton. The royalists put up strong resistance and just managed to retain the town but it was an indication of how far things had now swung against the king in Lancashire.

The Battle of Whalley April 1643

THE royalists' greatest setback came at Whalley on 20th April 1643. Most of the first civil war in Lancashire had been a struggle for the control of towns and castles conducted by means of siege, storm and battery, but Whalley was a field action and probably the most important of the first civil war in the county.

After taking Preston Lord Derby had advanced his army of about 5,000 up the Ribble towards Whalley, intending, it would appear, to march

east and south in a concerted attempt to subdue finally the parliamentarian hundreds of Blackburn and Salford. Accompanying him was the cream of Lancahire's royalist officers, including Lord Molyneux, Sir Gilbert Hoghton and Sir Thomas Tyldesley.

The parliamentarians initially fell back before this imposing force, but Colonel Shuttleworth gathered reinforcements at Gawthorpe Hall ready to oppose them. As the royalists left the Ribble and marched via Whalley in the direction of Padiham Shuttleworth's men took up defensive positions near Read Hall. As the royalist army marched out of the valley of the Sabden Brook they were caught completely by surprise by a well-aimed

Sir Thomas Tyldesley, the king's most loyal supporter in Lancashire. N.P.G.

volley from the parliamentarians. Such was the ensuing confusion and noise that what had begun as little more than an impromptu defensive manoeuvre by the parliamentarians turned into a rout. The royalist vanguard panicked and was precipitously pushed back down the slope. Tyldesley and others attempted to halt the retreat and put up a fight but were forced back by the relentless pressure. The royalists first fled back across the Ribble and then marched back to Preston.

Royalist fortunes continued to decline. Wigan was taken by Colonel Assheton; and Lord Derby, either fearing that the Isle of Man was under threat from a Scottish attack or thinking the king's cause already to have been lost in Lancashire, retreated there. Lancaster also fell and fourteen of the Spanish guns were finally carried away by the parliamentarians. By June Warrington, Thurland and Hornby were all reduced.

Mid-17th-century English 'mortuary' sword, so called because it was believed the cameo faces in the hilt represented the beheaded Charles I. York Castle Museum.

The first siege of Lathom House, 1644

THE parliamentarians were now in such a strong position that they could afford to send some troops out of the county to support their compatriots in Yorkshire and Cheshire where their cause was faring less well. In January 1644 a number of Lancashire troops took part in the battle of Nantwich, a resounding parliamentarian success that prevented all of Cheshire being overrun by the king's forces.

The last places to hold out for the king in Lancashire were Lathom House and Greenhalgh Castle. Lathom was held by Lord Derby's wife, the redoubtable Countess Charlotte de la Tremouille, and in February the Manchester Committee decided it should be besieged by Colonels Assheton, Rigby and Moore. Sir Thomas Fairfax, senior parliamentarian commander in the area, took charge and attempted to negotiate a surrender.

At first the Countess successfully played for time, taking full advantage of Sir Thomas's natural gallantry and willingness to let her and her children escape. Negotiation ended on March 11, when Fairfax's last offer was refused. This would have allowed all the garrison to depart with all their

No known contemporary depiction of the original Lathom House exists, but a written description of the house allowed a 19th-century artist to come up with this impression of what he thought it might have looked like. From Draper's 'House of Stanley', 1864.

weapons and goods on condition they would not fight again. Lady Charlotte, however, had decided to fight it out.

The defenders numbered about 300, under eight captains, whilst the attackers had nearly ten times that number at their disposal. These they used in rotation to man the siege lines and creep the trenches closer to the walls. Things began to go wrong for the parliamentarians very quickly; Sir Thomas was called away to Yorkshire

and on March 12th the defenders sallied out, surprising the besiegers and killing several, and the exercise was repeated on the 17th.

To keep the parliamentarians from getting too close, atop the towers of Lathom were placed:

The best and choicest marksmen, who usually attended the Earl in his hunting and other sports as Huntsmen, Keepers, Fowlers, and the like; who continually kept watch with scrued guns [rifles] and long

Fowling pieces . . . to the great Anoyance and loss of the Enemy, especially, of their Commanders, who were frequently killed in their trenches as they came and went from them.

A continuing problem was a large mortar deployed by the attackers that was capable of hurling 13-inch bombs or stones over the defences into the house. One of the mortar crew was shot by a sniper but the mortar caused considerable damage and began to undermine morale, as one commentator remarked, even the stoutest soldiers 'had noe hearts for grenadoes!'

The mortar was therefore targeted by the defenders for a sally. On 15th April they reached it but were driven off before they could nail the touch hole or smash it, but on a second attempt ten days later they captured the enemy gun, put it on a low 'dragge', and pulled it back to the house in triumph.

The besiegers now began to lose heart. Colonel Assheton was called away and the men in the trenches were constantly harrassed by the defenders. In May came the news that Prince Rupert had crossed the Mersey with a large force and the parliamentarians now had no option but to desist.

The redoubtable Countess Derby in later life. It was said that she had 'stolen the Earl's breeches' during her defence of Lathom. National Portrait Gallery.

Captain Charnock, one of Lathom's defenders. From Astley Hall, Chorley.

Prince Rupert in Lancashire, 1644

HAVING brushed aside some rather feeble resistance at Stockport Prince Rupert, one of the king's most experienced and able commanders, with almost 10,000 men proceeded to clear much of Lancashire. On 28th May he stormed Bolton where Colonel Rigby and his men had taken refuge. The first attack was beaten off but the Earl of Derby led in a second wave, in the words of one commentator 'killing all before them without any respect'. Estimates of the casualties vary but it seems that nearly a thousand died inside the town plus a couple of hundred of the attacking troops. The 'bloody and barbarous massacre at Bolton' caused a good deal of bitterness and became probably the most infamous incident in all of the civil wars in Lancashire. Lord Derby himself was accused of killing a parliamentarian captain after he had

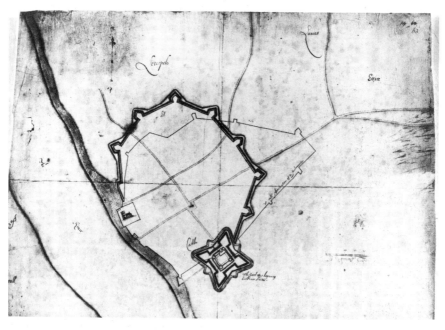

A contemporary plan of the proposed fortifications at Liverpool, in the Dutch style with projecting bastions linked by earth ramparts. Although only the defences marked by the faint line were actually built, the town was able to resist Rupert for a fortnight. Liverpool R.O.

surrendered, whilst it seems certain that women and children died as well as combatants. Twenty-two colours were taken and these were returned in triumph to Lathom.

Rupert avoided Manchester and now marched on Liverpool. This had stronger defences and resisted for two weeks under bombardment and storm. The defenders used wool sacks to block up holes in the walls and conceal their movements, but by a night assault at the north end of town the royalists finally broke in. Colonel Moore, the parliamentarian commander, and some others escaped by ship.

Prince Rupert's dashing campaign in Lancashire brought the county under royal control, but the decisive royalist defeat at Marston Moor reversed the tide of war once more and the parliamentarians were able to re-assert their control in Lancashire fairly quickly. This portrait of Rupert is by Gerard van Honthorst. National Portrait Gallery.

Marston Moor, 1644

NOW Rupert marched via Lathom into Yorkshire, taking with him some of the Lancashire royalists' best troops, including the regiments of Sir Thomas Tyldesley and Lord Molyneux. His objective was the relief of York which was besieged by a large allied parliamentarian–Scottish army under the command of Lords Leven, Fairfax and Manchester. Advancing from Skipton Rupert's army forced the allies to break off their seige whilst he slipped in to free York.

Rupert now made a controversial decision and pursued the numerically superior allied army, catching them at Marston Moor about six miles from the city on 2nd July 1644. In the biggest battle of the civil war 18,000 royalists attacked the 25,000 or so parliamentarians in a hard-fought evening struggle which resulted in Rupert's total defeat. The whole course of the war in the north of England was decisively affected and the battle brought to prominence a little known lieutenant general of cavalry, Oliver Cromwell. Rupert retreated rapidly west with only the remnants of what had been one of the largest royalist armies ever gathered. On 8th July he was at Hornby Castle and then he went south via Preston.

The parliamentarians now set about mopping up enemy forces in the county. A parliamentarian army under Sir John Meldrum retook Preston and pursued most of the remaining royalists out of the county, skirmishing with them at Ormskirk.

The siege of Lathom was renewed, Sir Thomas Tyldesley fled to Wales and Liverpool was starved into surrender. Greenhalgh Castle near Garstang was besieged by Colonels Doddington and Rigby and finally brought to surrender in June 1645.

Lathom, under the command this time of Colonels Rawsthorne and Kay, as well as a number of captains who had taken part in the first siege, held on doggedly.

With the king defeated at Naseby, and again at Rowton Heath, Charles sent word in September that the garrison should surrender. Even so it was not until 3rd December 1645 that they laid down their arms.

The second siege had none of the romance or glamour of the first. There was no Lady Derby conducting an heroic defence with several

Captain Kay, one of the royalist defenders during the second siege of Lathom House.

hundred soldiers; only a small band of die-hards whom the besiegers had to starve into surrender in the end.

The house itself was 'slighted' and nothing now remains of the building. Even its location is something of a mystery, with several sites competing for the honour; the most likely location is close to the site of the later Lathom House which itself is now ruinous. Little, therefore, can be seen today of the site of one of the most romantic episodes of the civil wars.

Five

THE SECOND CIVIL WAR

DURING the early part of 1646 Charles I was defeated all over the country. The king himself surrendered to the Scots at Newark on 5th May and they in their turn gave him up to parliament. Yet there was no diplomatic solution and now tensions were beginning to rise between parliament and the army they had 'new modelled' in 1644–5. There was not enough money to pay off the arrears of money owing to the troops and the expensive army was proving difficult to disband.

In June 1647 Cornet Joyce seized the royal prisoner on behalf of the army and took him from Holdenby House to Newmarket. Now the army itself was riven by internal dispute. 'Agitators' called for a new system of government as well as back pay; mutiny broke out in some regiments and force was used to reimpose order. Charles, who had escaped once and was now held at Carisbrooke on the Isle of Wight, now signed a secret 'engagement' with the Scots promising that presbyterianism would be introduced in England for a trial period if they would support him.

Revolt also broke out in South Wales in February and Cromwell hurried off there with the New Model. The Scots began to raise an army and there were outbreaks of disorder in Kent, East Anglia and elsewhere.

The Preston campaign 1648

WHILE Fairfax was engaged with the rebels in Kent and Essex the Scots army crossed the northern border. Lancashire parliamentarians immediately tried to raise forces for the defence of the county. Colonel Assheton was their commander-in-chief, with regiments commanded by Rigby, Doddington, Standish and two of the Shuttleworth family, but the total number of men under arms probably did not exceed 2,000. These were moved north in July to rendezvous with Major General Lambert at Carlisle.

At first it was believed that the Scots would push south down the eastern side of the country but as Lambert manoeuvred to cover this possibility Hamilton's army struck through Westmorland. The Scottish advance was slow but Cromwell, detailed to reinforce Lambert, moved rapidly: the main body of the New Model joined Lambert and the Lancashire parliamentarians on 13 August 1648 near Wetherby.

Although outnumbered, Cromwell was determined to fight as soon as possible. He advanced his 9,000 men via Skipton and Clitheroe to Stonyhurst where he spent the night of August 16th. Local tradition has it that he slept on the dining table in fear of his life from the local Catholics; more probably he fell asleep *at* the table, perhaps after writing his report to parliament.

In the meantime the main Scottish army was straggling down through Lancaster in the direction of Preston. The Duke of Hamilton was in overall command, with Lt. General Callender in charge of the cavalry (which had already advanced to near Wigan in the hope of better foraging), and Munro with Ulster Scots in the rear. Marmaduke Lord Langdale, a prominent Yorkshire royalist, covered the advance on the east. Despite the Scottish slowness Langdale was in good spirits, writing to the royalist Sir Charles Lucas that

In this our march towards Preston, we feare no overtures. Heavy taxes and grevious quarterings have made many already shake off the insupportable yoak of their slavery. The farther we go, the more confident we are!'

The Scots and royalists did have good reason for optimism. The Scots numbered about 18,000 and Langdale's force about another 4,000 and they therefore outnumbered Cromwell's army by at least two to one.

Langdale and Cromwell's advance guard first clashed on the Preston–Longridge road near Ribbleton, not far from where Langdale had spent the night, at Grimsargh, whilst the Scots, widely strung out up the Lancaster road, were beginning to pass through Preston. Cromwell quickly deployed his main force and set to with Langdale, achieving a local

Lieutenant General Oliver Cromwell, whose Preston campaign in 1648 was one of the most brilliant military actions of the wars. Contemporary painting after Robert Walker. National Portrait Gallery.

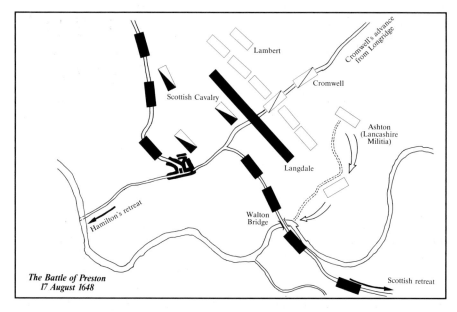

The Battle of Preston
17 August 1648

superiority. Hamilton refused to believe that this was the main body of the New Model and, largely ignoring Langdale's appeals for support, continued his march.

Langdale put up a spirited fight but in the course of the afternoon he was pushed back from his position on Eaves Brook back towards the town. While Cromwell's main force dispatched and scattered the last of Langdale's command and began to close on the town, Assheton's Lancashire contingent outflanked the royalists by advancing down Watery Lane to the Ribble Bridge. The Scottish force was now effectively cut in two and scattered in all directions.

Hamilton gathered part of his army on Walton Hill, which they managed to hold during the evening despite the loss of their baggage train to Cromwell's advanced guard. During the night they resolved on retreat, hoping to rendezvous further south with the bulk of their cavalry under General Middleton. They failed to meet and Hamilton, now reduced to about half his original strength, straggled on to Wigan, harried by enemy cavalry.

Bad weather, lack of supplies and the relentlessness of the pursuit all took their toll. A last stand was made at Winwick near Warrington before most of the remaining Scots surrendered. Small groups and fugitives continued to be found and captured for a week afterwards, as far south as Uttoxeter.

Six

THE EXECUTION OF THE KING AND THE THIRD CIVIL WAR

PRESTON had been the most important as well as the biggest battle of the second civil war. Fairfax defeated the Kent rebels at Maidstone and last resistance ceased at Colchester on 24th August when news was heard of the battle at Preston.

Military victory in 1648 solved no more than that in 1646 but opinion had hardened against the king, who had been beaten in the field, offered fair terms, and then started a new war while negotiating peace. Parliament was purged by the army and the king stood trial and was executed in January 1649. Fairfax did not approve of these proceedings but there was little he could do, and he was replaced by Cromwell as Lord General the next year. Cromwell now put down unrest in the army and proceeded to pacify Ireland.

In Lancashire the local militia was disbanded with the aid of a £1,444 payment. Only a couple of small units refused to disband but these were forcibly repressed by Major General Assheton and Colonel Duckenfield on the instructions of parliament.

In June 1650 Charles Stuart, son of Charles I landed in Scotland. Cromwell immediately launched a Scottish campaign, realising that this move could only mean that a new invasion of England was planned. By the middle of 1651 it was clear that Cromwell had gained the upper hand in Scotland and Charles and the Scottish general Leslie resolved on the gamble of an attack into England.

In August 1651 Lancashire was again invaded by the Scots. Charles was proclaimed king at Penrith on 7th and at Lancaster on 11th August. The council of state ordered two parliamentary Major Generals – Lambert and Harrison – to contain the new king's advance. Lambert with his cavalry dogged them from the rear whilst Harrison waited south of the Ribble. There was a skirmish near Warrington but the royal army managed to get through to Cheshire.

King Charles receiving the heavenly crown of glory in exchange for the earthly crown of vanity, from the 'Eikon Basilike'.

In the meantime Lord Derby, named as the king's 'General in Lancashire', had landed at Preesall sands having finally left his stronghold in the Isle of Man. After a council of war at Warrington Derby began recruiting on behalf of the king; the leaders present included Lord Widdrington, Sir Thomas Tyldesley, Sir William Throgmorton, Sir Francis Gamul and half a dozen well-known colonels.

Lord Derby's enterprise was ill-fated from the start, for Colonels Lilburne and Charles Worsley (later Cromwell's Major General for the North West) were quickly detailed to deal with this new threat. The royalists, numbering perhaps 1,500, gathered at Preston and Lilburne with cavalry of the New Model encamped at Brindle to cover them. Skirmishes occurred on August 22nd and August 23rd. Lilburne then fell back to Hoghton to await reinforcement.

The royalists now thought their best chance of success lay with a rapid march south taking Worsley's infantry by surprise before he could join Lilburne. The parliamentarians realised next morning that Derby's force was on the move and followed up, catching the royalists near Wigan on 25th August.

Despite the small numbers involved the battle was fierce in the cramped lanes and hedges. Though Lord Derby escaped, some of his best supporters were killed, including Widdrington, Throgmorton and the irrepressible Sir Thomas Tyldesley, who was unhorsed and shot. Derby, slightly wounded, fled south to join Charles at Worcester.

Here came the final disaster. On September 3rd Cromwell led the main body of the New Model to attack the town from more than one direction. Charles and his Scottish and English supporters were comprehensively defeated.

Lord Derby was again a fugitive; harried by enemy cavalry he finally surrendered to a Lancashire captain called Oliver Edge and was taken off to Chester. There he was tried for treason and convicted. Despite several appeals he was executed at Bolton on October 16th, 1651.

The legacy of civil war

THE short-term effects of nearly a decade of intermittent warfare were considerable. There had been significant death and destruction, England had become a republic and the once powerful House of Lords was abolished. The cost of armies was high and, while the war continued, many local matters were dealt with by locally imposed 'committees'. Many royalists were fined or had their estates 'sequestered' but few, like Lord Derby, paid the ultimate price.

Half-crown showing Oliver Cromwell as Lord Protector in the year of his death, 'warts and all'. A. Miles.

When the wars were over there were experiments with military rule, the 'rump' of the long parliament and finally 'protectorate' under first Oliver and then Richard Cromwell.

In the Church there were no bishops and a 'Directory of Public Worship' replaced the Book of Common Prayer. Altars, pictures and 'superstitious inscriptions' were also largely swept away. Attempts were also made to suppress the use of Latin, not only in religion but in law and government and replace it with English. There were effects on popular culture, too; there was an attempt to ban Christmas and there was a crackdown on alehouses. Lancashire had more than its fair share of these, and Clitheroe in particular had one for every 15 inhabitants.

Longer term effects were more subtle, as many of the changes of the 1640s and 1650s were reversed at the Restoration, and there was no radical redistribution of land and property. Some of the bastions of localism had been broken down and king and army were viewed in a new light.

In the summer of 1659 there was another upsurge of royalism in Cheshire and south Lancashire and a rising by Sir George Booth which was quelled by General Lambert. Ironically it was only a year later that the army under General Monck was instrumental in the restoration of Charles II.

Further reading

The best single-volume history of the English civil wars is R. Ashton's *The English Civil War* (1983), whilst for Lancashire Ernest Broxap's *The Great Civil War in Lancashire* (Manchester, 1910) is still the best survey. The Battle of Preston is covered by R. Holmes, *The Battle of Preston, 1648* (Market Drayton, 1985).

Any study of the Lancashire civil wars must use as its starting point the *Civil War Tracts*, published by the Chetham Society (volume ii) in 1844, and the *Discourse of the Warr in Lancashire* (Chetham Society, 1864).

For the social background, see B. G. Blackwood, *The Lancashire Gentry and the Great Rebellion* (Chetham Society, 1978); and John Walton, *Lancashire: A Social History* (Manchester, 1987)

There is a large number of books on the various military aspects of the wars, including Firth's *Cromwell's Army* (London, 1902).